TIMELESS
Images

ARIZONA
HIGHWAYS BOOK

TIMELESS
Images

Text — Robert C. Dyer

Photography — *Arizona Highways* Contributors

Photography Editor — J. Peter Mortimer

Text Editor — Dean Smith

Art Director — Gary Bennett

Production Manager — Cindy Mackey

Production — Christine Mitchell and Mary W. Velgos

Prepared by the Related Products Section of
Arizona Highways magazine, a publication of the
Arizona Department of Transportation. Hugh Harelson,
Publisher; Wesley Holden, Managing Editor;
Robert J. Farrell, Associate Editor.

Library of Congress Catalog Number 89-081819
ISBN 0-916179-27-3

TABLE
of
CONTENTS

The Formative Years 6

The Tradition Grows 66

Images to Match a Timeless Land *110*

THE FORMATIVE
Years

Photography is an art, an important art which our own decades have done so much to perfect, an art which has added so much to the broad field of culture. The photographer cannot replace the painter, but he can supplement his work. If we will stop and think for a moment, we will realize and appreciate what photography means to us. It brings the world into our homes. Through photography we know our world better; and better we know ourselves and our neighbors.

Photography is the medium which we use in this publication each month to bring you the absorbing story of Arizona and the Southwest . . .

Desert thunderstorm near Tucson was included in a photo-feature, "The Dramatic Skies of Arizona" (June 1979).
RAY MANLEY

The editor of *Arizona Highways* magazine wrote those words some three decades after the publication made its second shaky entrance into the publishing world. By the time of his writing, there was no longer any doubt that the youngster would survive and flourish; it was an appropriate time to redefine and redirect it, to state its mission.

Also by that time (September 1955), *Arizona Highways* had established a firm claim to eminence, perhaps pre-eminence, among nationally known consumer magazines in the area of four-color photographic reproduction. In fact, the development of full-color photography in periodicals and the growth of *Arizona Highways* into the most successful and most admired magazine of its type are so intertwined that the story of one is inevitably the story of the other.

By name only, the history of *Arizona Highways* might be traced to the debut in 1921, in less-than-modest circumstances, of what today would be referred to as no more than a newsletter. There was nothing in it to tell a historian that "this is where it all began," and its hold on life was brief.

The real genesis of today's *Arizona Highways* was in April 1925, when the State Highway Department began publication of a sort of gazette, in magazine format, to tell the small-but-growing motoring public where the newest roads, bridges, and culverts were being built for their convenience and safety.

Early editors of that unpretentious journal found opportunities to place occasional black-and-white photos of scenic Arizona among the articles on road building and bridge design. After all, someone reasoned, roads meant travel, travel meant tourists, tourists liked scenery, etc. Moreover, if the magazine published a picture of a bridge, then why not show the stream, and the mountains where the stream rose?

Several editors sneaked in such pictures, but with the arrival in 1938 of the sixth in their succession, Raymond Carlson, the man unanimously credited with guiding the magazine to greatness,

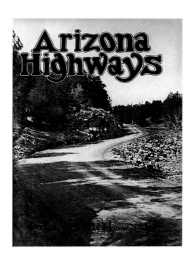

Arizona Highways could be said truly to have had, if not a new birth, then certainly a rebirth.

One person who received an early hint of Carlson's vision was Josef Muench, whose name eventually was to become synonymous with western scenic photography. An immigrant gardener whose education had been halted by the rigors of World War I in Germany, Muench had a love for photography and a love for Arizona growing from his first visit here in 1936.

Two years after seeing Arizona for the first time, he saw his first copy of *Arizona Highways* in a Phoenix service station. The inside photos were of highway construction, but the scenic cover picture caught Muench's eye. On his next visit to Arizona, he brought with him a box of 8 by 10 black-and-white prints—images he had taken on visits to the state, processed and printed in his own darkroom in Santa Barbara, California.

"I held them almost religiously in my hands," says Muench, remembering his nervous call on Carlson in the little shack behind the Arizona Highway Department headquarters in Phoenix that served as the editor's office. Muench didn't know it, but Carlson had been in his job only one month.

"I was like a lost little boy trying to make a business deal. He was trying to get something out of me while I was trying to get something out of him.

"He went through the prints, all 50 of them, turning them over one at a time. Finally he said, 'This is what I want to bring this magazine to. Can I keep these?'"

Eventually all 50 images were seen by readers of *Arizona Highways*. That was an exclusive group at the time; Muench recalls that only 3,400 copies of each issue were being printed.

One of the first of the impressive roster of contributing photographers and writers developed by Carlson (in all its 65 years, *Arizona Highways* has had only one "staff" photographer), Muench must be numbered among the "founding fathers" of *Arizona Highways* photography. Also in that elite group were Esther Henderson, Ray Manley, Ansel Adams, Carlos Elmer, Chuck Abbott, Hubert Lowman, Herb and Dorothy McLaughlin, Barry Goldwater, Joseph McGibbeny, Wayne Davis, Norman G. Wallace, and perhaps a few others.

Among those early imagemakers there were also Forman Hanna, a Globe pharmacist and an outstanding photographer, and Norman Rhoads Garrett of Prescott. Hanna and Garrett are the only members of the roster who were fellows of the (British) Royal Photographic Society, although Goldwater and Muench were associates.

Individualists all, they nonetheless shared a vision at a time and in a place that was propitious to the development of *Arizona Highways*. In turn, the magazine and its editor, complemented by the design talents of George Avey in those formative years, provided an outlet for the work of those photographers, appreciative of their best and demanding better. It was a synergistic relationship that resulted in a fantastic growth in circulation and readership and a worldwide fame unmatched by any publication of similar purpose or scope.

According to many, including Herb McLaughlin, who has had

(LEFT) "Day's End in Navajoland" was photographed on a midwinter day in Monument Valley (December 1957).

RAY MANLEY

(INSET) Cover of first issue depicted a roadway near Prescott (April 1925).

(FOLLOWING PANEL, PAGES 10 AND 11) Twilight over Joshua trees on the Mohave Desert (June 1979).

JOSEF MUENCH

hundreds of images published in the magazine, there is no doubt that *Arizona Highways* played a major role in the development of color photography in the magazine field.

"Go back to the first color, in the late 1930s and early '40s," McLaughlin says. "Rare was the magazine that printed even a color cover. For a long time *National Geographic* used black-and-white and *Arizona Highways* used color."

Willis Peterson, a photographer, writer, and teacher who has studied the magazine through the years as well as contributing to it, adds: "Start back in the old magazines, with the rough paper they were printed on; color photography and *Arizona Highways* are synonymous."

Muench asserts unequivocally that, in the use of color, *Arizona Highways* was soon "leading the way—particularly in nature subjects." Along with himself, he lists Manley, Henderson, and Herb McLaughlin among the photographers who were heavily involved in moving the magazine into color.

Actually, the first full color photograph used by the magazine was a view of lower Oak Creek Canyon by Norman G. Wallace, used on the cover of the July 1938 issue. Wallace, a locating engineer for the Highway Department, took along a view camera while working in the field, bringing back images to help fulfill the new vision of *Arizona Highways*. For this cover, he used Kodachrome film, which had been on the market only a few years.

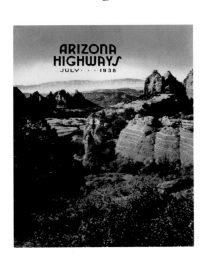

Carlson took due note of the innovative cover in his "Neighborly Notes" column, asking: ". . . how can we, through the medium of black and white, paint a picture of the gold in an Arizona sunset, portray the blue of an Arizona sky, tell the fiery red and green of an Arizona desert in bloom?" But it was five months before *Arizona Highways* tried another four-color cover, this one a Grand Canyon view credited to G. E. Ruckstell of Boulder City, Nevada.

How the first four-color cover came about is a story apparently lost. Neither Carlson nor Wallace nor George Avey is alive to tell it. Avey's son Gary, who grew up on the folklore of *Arizona Highways* and became its editor (1980-83), doesn't recall hearing who proposed the idea or what obstacles might have been overcome to make it a reality. Because it appeared about six months after Carlson became editor, and considering the lead time required for such a venturesome project, it is easy to believe that Carlson made four-color process printing a goal right from the beginning of his tenure.

"I think I was the first to bring in color," says Muench. Carlson didn't have the right kind of light to see the true colors in Muench's 4 by 5 transparencies, "but it didn't take him long to become prepared."

However pleasant it might be to see that July 1938 color cover as a launching pad for *Arizona Highways'* greatest period of growth, the fact is that it is mainly of historical interest. The magazine really began to soar only after World War II.

As *Arizona Highways* challenged photographers to improve their images, taking advantage of developments in print reproduction, its contributing photographers were raising their own standards. At times they pushed the magazine to explore

new ways to reproduce on paper the full, rich palette of color that camera artists were capturing on transparencies. One photographer likened it to "a matched pair pulling a wagon; both working together."

Wayne Davis, whose familiarity with Canyon de Chelly as a government agricultural specialist translated into countless *Arizona Highways* images of that spectacular area and its Indian inhabitants, gives the magazine credit for improving the overall quality of photography. "Its excellence encouraged us to pull ourselves up by our bootstraps and improve our work."

About the time that Josef Muench made his first appearance in the magazine, Carlson also was corralling the talents of a young Phoenix businessman and amateur photographer named Barry Goldwater to help steer *Arizona Highways* toward the future that he foresaw.

The first of nearly 300 images Goldwater has had published in *Arizona Highways* came about after a chance encounter at an informal opening for the old Apache Brewing Co. Carlson asked Goldwater if he had any photographs he might use. The first one selected was a scene of Coal Mine Canyon, between Tuba City and Oraibi.

The future U.S. senator's interest in the magazine developed into a fine collection of back issues, dating back to 1925, the magazine's first year. He also was a keen observer of *Arizona Highways*' emergence into greatness.

"Carlson was more than an editor," Goldwater says. "He was a poet. He looked on pictures as poetry. He looked on *Arizona Highways* as poetry."

If those early photographers recruited by Carlson praise the editor to the skies, the editor knew what was required of a photographer. His words, from the September 1955 issue:

The lucky shot, taken haphazardly, may, and often does, result in a superior picture. The photographer, however, who comes up with the good ones regularly cannot depend on luck alone. He must first of all master the tools of his trade. (Too many would-be photographers, alas! fail to do that.) He must be industrious, patient, enthusiastic, poetic, philosophic, lucky to an extent, imaginative, discerning, critical and possessed of an eye which appreciates the beautiful, the dramatic and the different. The consistently good photographer, above all, must be prepared to work hard, which means going back for the good ones. The rewards may not be great, but there is always satisfaction in a good picture and there is always fun.

The rewards, in fact, (those measured in financial terms) were not that great for those photographers who participated in lifting *Arizona Highways* to its artistic heights. The late Ansel Adams, listed among the greats in world photography, shared in the penurious pay scale along with everyone else.

"Ansel was a great fan of the magazine," says Carlos Elmer, one of the foremost contributors to the golden age of *Arizona Highways*' growth, and still an active photographer-writer-publisher. "Long after he commanded high prices, he was very happy to let *Arizona Highways* have color for $35."

For years, *Arizona Highways* shared with *Desert* magazine the dubious distinction of being the poorest paying markets for photographers working in their general area of interest, according to Elmer.

Herb McLaughlin, who arrived in Phoenix in 1945 and called on Carlson in his tiny adobe office next to the railroad tracks, remembers that the early pay scale was "about two or three dollars for a black-and-white; five or 10 dollars for color. A cover

(LEFT) A monsoon storm creates special effects on the high desert near St. Johns (August 1986). WAYNE DAVIS (FOLLOWING PANEL, PAGES 18 AND 19) Apache cattle drive on the reservation, included in "Special All-Cowboy Issue" (February 1980). RAY MANLEY

(RIGHT) "Autumn Campfire."
Photographed near the Circle Z Ranch in
the Patagonia area in mid-November, this
front cover image introduced an article
titled, "Autumn—From Mountains to
Desert " (October 1957).
RAY MANLEY

(ABOVE) "Sundown on the Big Sandy Wash
and Liar's Hour Begins"; photographed on
the Dave Ericsson Ranch (February 1980).
RAY MANLEY

ARIZONA
HIGHWAYS
APRIL • 1955
THIRTY-FIVE CENTS

was a big deal—about 25 or 30 dollars."

Why did these photographers, who came to command significantly higher prices in other markets, always turn to *Arizona Highways*?

Ray Manley, for example. From a Boy Scout merit badge in photography to worldwide assignments that kept him on the go for months at a time, Manley has always remained a familiar name to *Arizona Highways* readers. Once he figured that he was spending as much as $100 to take an image which he would sell to *Arizona Highways* for only a fifth that amount.

"It was a great benefit to a photographer," says Manley. "It was great publicity and a good credit line." Other photographers agree.

"You did it for the love of the magazine, and for love of the country," McLaughlin remembers. But another photographer reminded that the magazine "was also a catalog of what you could do," providing publicity and recognition for those whose work it published.

That dichotomous feeling permeates the attitudes of many photographers toward the magazine. There is the *Arizona Highways* that recognizes, loves, and nurtures their art, to the extent that pay seems almost incidental. And there is the *Arizona Highways* that, in cold business terms, has become such an international success that it functions as a salesman working for them in other, higher-paying territories.

In the words of Allan C. Reed, whose background as a graphic designer and advertising executive enabled him to lay out some of his own pages in *Arizona Highways*, the magazine is simply "the epitome of photography."

Carlos Elmer suggests from his own experience that hopeful photographers eyeing the *Arizona Highways* market in those days fared better if they took pictures as a sideline away from a regular job. "I was an engineering instrumentation photographer; Esther Henderson was a dancer, then ran a portrait studio; Ray Manley free-lanced and did commercial photography."

Henderson had been a professional dancer, it's true, but she selected photography school deliberately as her exit visa from the world of show business. Photography "dealt with line and light—two factors I was familiar with as a dancer." Henderson came west to Tucson from New York City and concentrated on building up her portrait studio business. Nevertheless, she was one of the first photographers actively recruited by Carlson in his search for scenic images of Arizona.

Her father assured Carlson that Esther had plenty of Arizona scenes on file, and would shoot any others he wanted, even doing it free. Brushing aside her protests, he told his daughter: "Listen, kiddo, that young fellow is going places, and you just tag along and you'll get there too."

Henderson did far more than just tag along, of course, becoming one of the leaders in *Arizona Highways'* stable of free-lance contributors. Not only were her black-and-white scenics a mainstay of the magazine for years, but she helped lead

(LEFT) "Aunt Eller's Farm." Arizona's San Rafael Valley provided the scenic setting, and Hollywood provided barn, windmill, smokehouse, and fence for filming of the motion picture, *Oklahoma!* Front cover introduced Reed's photo story inside (April 1955). ALLEN C. REED

(ABOVE) "Old Chloride," 25 miles north of Kingman in the Cerbat Mountains. Window of an old shack framed Tennessee Mine and Mill structures for feature on ghost towns of Arizona (August 1960). CARLOS ELMER

the transition into color photography. Her unusual view of San Xavier Mission was *Arizona Highways'* third four-color cover, introducing the 1939 Christmas issue. A year later, her scene of San Francisco Peaks was the magazine's fourth venture into four-color process.

With Henderson's color work on the front, that 1940 Christmas issue was another major milestone in *Arizona Highways'* development as the leader in color reproduction. A 12-page color portfolio captioned "Colorful Arizona . . . An Adventure in Beauty" showcased 20 color photos by Max Kegley, the first use of full color photography inside the magazine.

Kegley, a rodeo photographer who also did scenic work, was the only person ever employed by *Arizona Highways* specifically to take pictures. Covering virtually the full range of scenes for which the magazine had already captured attention in black-and-white photography, Kegley in effect forecast the years to come in *Arizona Highways* color: two scenes of the Grand Canyon, the Navajo Indian Fair, Boulder Dam, saguaro blossoms, ocotillo in bloom, San Xavier Mission, Monument Valley, Oak Creek Canyon, saguaros silhouetted against a flaming sunset, and more.

Henderson recalls the transition from black-and-white film to color as "gradually, but rather fast." Her late husband, Chuck

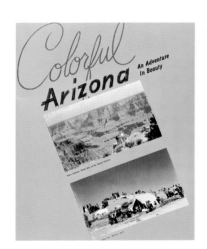

Abbott, also a frequent contributor to *Arizona Highways*, was insisting in the early 1940s that both should be shooting more color.

"In either 1941 or 1942, we had a very colorful year. Roosevelt Dam filled for the very first time, and down by Picacho Peak the wildflowers were knee high. I decided that we would shoot one box of color to every five boxes of black-and-white. In just a few years the ratio would be five to one in reverse. The change came very quickly."

The cost of color film made photographers highly selective in their use of it. Josef Muench, who has consistently used the 4 by 5 format for professional work, remembers buying Kodachrome cut film, 10 sheets to a box, and husbanding each sheet carefully. In those days, he says, "I still shot black-and-white about 10 to one over color."

"You had to have a market for color," says Hubert A. Lowman, a former Kansas Citian who fell in love with the Southwest, "blundered" into photography and broke into *Arizona Highways* in 1941.

Lowman, now semiretired in California, made *Arizona Highways'* front cover with the first color image he sold to the publication, a sunset lavishly colored with gold and pink, as background for a stand of saguaro cactus.

The decision of Eastman Kodak in the late 1940s to discontinue Kodachrome cut film, following its successful introduction of Ektachrome, still rankles many photographers. Under any conditions, they say, the colors in Ektachrome transparencies fade over time. When picture editors linger too long over the light table with precious images, the labors, the inspiration, and the artistic talents of photographers become victims. And the process of making color separations also speeds the loss of color, although modern laser scanners are less destructive.

Muench, who keeps his transparencies in metal cabinets under

(INSET) "Colorful Arizona . . . An Adventure in Beauty" was a landmark in *Arizona Highways* history: 20 color images in a 12-page portfolio marking its first use of full color on inside pages. Photos on opening page are of Point Sublime, on the North Rim of the Grand Canyon, and the Navajo Fair at Window Rock (December 1940).
MAX KEGLEY

(FAR LEFT) "Ear of the Wind Arch" in Monument Valley. Just as photographer Reed was preparing to shoot this scene, the horse spooked, threw its Indian woman rider, and dragged her at a gallop, one foot caught in the stirrup. Reed and trader Harry Goulding were able to head off the horse and save the woman from serious injury or death. She insisted on remounting for the photo, but a gentler horse was used (April 1956).
ALLEN C. REED

(LEFT) "The Patient" was pictured
during a rare opportunity to observe and
photograph a Navajo medicine man
treating this woman. Because her child
was still nursing, he was considered part
of her body and also participated
in the ceremony (July 1947).
J. H. McGIBBENY

(ABOVE) "Navajo Sing." Gathering of
tribal members for a ceremonial
occasioned by a member's illness would
last for several days (August 1946).
MAX KEGLEY

(RIGHT) "The Bride" was included in a
picture story on the Hopi people, entitled
"Children of the Sun" (July 1947).
J. H. McGIBBENY

(ABOVE) "Hopi Dance" was part
of the same feature, "Children of the Sun"
(July 1947). J.H. McGIBBENY

ARIZONA HIGHWAYS

controlled temperature conditions, says flatly that "fluorescent light is a devil to your film."

Because of the resale market so critical to the financial success of photographers, the unavailability of large-format Kodachrome, coupled with the discovery that Ektachrome was not forever, was a serious matter.

"It was a tragedy," says Carlos Elmer. "In many cases, the work of years is gone."

The loss may depend largely on the type of image, notes photographer Jerry Jacka. "In my case, it's especially a problem with Indian portraits and much of the Indian art. I'm not concerned with the loss of scenic images. You still have to keep shooting scenery and improving anyway. That is one assignment that is never completed."

Reuse of images was and is important to *Arizona Highways* photographers. The importance was multiplied for those whose work in the formative years brought them small cash payments from a magazine that had bravely decided to do without the advertising revenues which pay the way for other magazines. Of equal importance is the way that exposure of their work in *Arizona Highways* has led to other opportunities, whether resale of the same images or expanded uses involving related subject matter—books, calendars, even museum exhibitions.

A prime example of reuse is a Grand Canyon sunrise scene, a portion of which first appeared 15 years ago as an *Arizona Highways* full page. Since then, photographer Josef Muench has sold use of the image 41 times. *Sunset* has used it twice, once in the magazine and again in a book, *Reader's Digest* books used it and it has even been on a billboard.

In the early days of four-color advertising, says Hubert Lowman, agencies were reluctant to spend their clients' money on expensive reproduction with uncertain results. "But an advertiser could buy rights to reprint a picture from *Arizona Highways* and know that he had something good, something that would reproduce well."

Barry Goldwater, who never considered himself more than an amateur photographer in spite of an excellent reputation and many sales, picked up additional income from his exposure in *Arizona Highways*. "The most popular," he says, "was an old Navajo. I've been paid up to $3,000 for that one." Like most of his work, the Navajo portrait was in black-and-white. Goldwater admittedly "never got too fond of color."

Expanded markets resulting directly from their *Arizona Highways* exposure have been important to photographers.

In the case of Ray Manley of Tucson, both the reputation and the activity have become worldwide. Inspired by Esther Henderson's early color images in *Arizona Highways*, Manley had set a career path that was interrupted by World War II service as a Navy photographer. His first postwar sale to *Arizona Highways*, he admits, was a photo of a cattle chute in Kansas that looked enough like the area around Willcox, Arizona, to achieve full-page publication. But his Arizona scenic images earned justifiable renown, and he became

(LEFT) An editor's note on this cover image said: "The Kodachromes in this issue are dedicated to our good neighbors. They were taken by Esther Henderson and Chuck Abbott, of Tucson, during a six-week camera tour of Mexico for *Arizona Highways*" (October 1945).
ESTHER HENDERSON

(ABOVE) A winter afternoon at Jokake Inn, a Scottsdale resort, helped illustrate a special tourism issue called "Fun in the Sun" (September 1947).
HERB McLAUGHLIN

(LEFT) The memory of a saguaro cactus
forest that no longer exists, north of
Phoenix off Interstate 17 near Carefree
Highway, is preserved in "An Arizona
Trademark" (January 1976).
DOROTHY McLAUGHLIN
(BELOW) Yucca and staghorn cholla cactus
against a sunset were captured on film by
Lowman near Wickenburg for his feature,
"Confessions of a Free Lancer" (February
1954). HUBERT A. LOWMAN

(FOLLOWING PANEL, PAGES 34 AND 35)
The spectacular "Morning Sun Over the
Grand Canyon" has been reprinted more
than 40 times since it was published in
Arizona Highways. It has appeared in
other magazines, in books, and even on a
billboard (December 1971).
JOSEF MUENCH

a familiar name to *Arizona Highways* readers around the world.

Approached for a photo-mural project associated with the Scandinavian Airlines exhibit at the 1958 Brussels World's Fair, Manley spent 3 1/2 months and $19,000 photographing European scenes only to see the deal fall through. But the scenes sold to individual clients, enabling Manley to break even in a year and a half—and they're still selling.

All the time continuing to shoot for *Arizona Highways*, Manley parlayed the experience into additional world photography expeditions and tours, a business that overshadows the commercial photography business that once was his bread and butter. His son, Alan, now operates the business and finds time to contribute images to *Arizona Highways*.

Through his combined talents, Willis Peterson has turned out a series on public television, and has written and photographed for books published by the Audubon Society, *Reader's Digest*, and *National Wildlife*. His "The Glory of Nature's Form" exhibit toured museums across the nation, and his article on Mount McKinley, originally published in *Audubon Magazine*, was selected by *Reader's Digest* as one of only 60 to make up its *America the Beautiful* scenic book published in 1970.

Another contributor whose work has led him into the world of books is Jerry Jacka. Influenced by a still life with Indian artifacts, on an *Arizona Highways* cover, the Arizona native had occasional—"and I really mean occasional!" —images published in the magazine until, in his late 30s, he junked a career in forensic photography in order to free-lance.

Spurred on, critiqued, and encouraged by Joe Stacey, then *Arizona Highways* editor, Jacka produced a color portfolio on prehistoric Indian artifacts that dominated the February 1974 issue. After another full issue on Indian baskets, Jacka was contacted by a book publisher. Seven books later, Jacka also has five complete issues of *Arizona Highways* to his credit, some including text written by his wife, Lois.

"It all happened in about two years; from an unheard-of photographer, I was put on the stage. We're just two Arizona kids who grew up near New River. None of this would have happened without *Arizona Highways*."

Unusual niches in the world of photography have helped earn livelihoods for many *Arizona Highways* imagemakers.

Peterson's communications skills brought him a proposal, in 1968, to set up a photography program at the not-yet-opened Glendale Community College. He had just time, before the school opened its doors, to plan the courses and bolster his teaching credentials with a master's degree. During his teaching career, he turned out a number of well-known professionals and added recognition as Arizona Journalism Teacher of the Year to many other professional awards.

Allen Reed, the designer-turned-photographer, first made the pages of *Arizona Highways* not as a photographer but as a layout artist. Arizona artist Ted DeGrazia, now famous but then unknown, was not a favorite of art editor George Avey. So Carlson asked Reed to lay out an article on DeGrazia.

(LEFT) "Monument Valley" illustrated an issue devoted to "Navajo County, Arizona, U.S.A.; Land of mesas, mountains, national parks, monuments and people who are proud of their land" (July 1970). BARRY GOLDWATER

(ABOVE) "Many Goats," portrait of a Navajo medicine man, was included in a portfolio entitled "Land of the People," with photographs by Goldwater and paintings by W. R. Leigh (July 1952). BARRY GOLDWATER (FOLLOWING PANEL, PAGES 38 AND 39) This scene of Navajos filling their canteens near Tuba City cutoff helped tell the story of the land and the people along U.S. 89 through Arizona (March 1957). RAY MANLEY

(LEFT) "Navajo" helped introduce "Colorful People," an article on Indians of the Southwest. Noted for black-and-white images, the photographer was represented in the same issue by scenic panoramas in color (December 1953).
ANSEL ADAMS

(ABOVE) "Old Man," appeared in an issue devoted to Navajos and Apaches. The caption read: "The years bring wisdom to the Navajo. The aged are held in high esteem and respect. Their voices are heard in the affairs of the tribe and their counsel considered. The years bring experience and worldly knowledge. With that comes dignity" (August 1946). RAY MANLEY

When another writer-photographer returned from an expedition with a batch of film ruined by heat, Reed shot pictures to accompany the article. His relationship with *Arizona Highways* flourished and, for a time, the advertising world lost a good account executive.

Hubert Lowman remarks that for some of his best work he received no credit at all—and not much money. For the first year or two after Disneyland opened, all the picture postcards on sale were Lowman's work. "Some awfully good pictures, too. But Disney was really chintzy; he paid $25 a shot for the ones he bought. Of course I took three times that many."

Lowman, like Josef Muench, was one of those rarities who walked into the *Arizona Highways* office with a bundle of his work and went on to participate in the development of a great magazine.

Inspired by newspaper rotogravure work of the noted Ray Atkeson, Lowman spent a year printing and mounting the images he had photographed vacationing in the Southwest. He took literally "a sackful" of prints to Carlson, "and I was in."

"My first cover was a picture I didn't even take," Lowman admits. "We were on the North Rim of the Grand Canyon, before the railings were put up, and I wanted my wife to sit on the edge, there at Bright Angel Point, so she would be in the picture.

"But she couldn't do it. I was using a tripod anyway; I had to use an exposure of about a tenth or maybe even a half a second. So I sat on the edge and had my wife pull the cable release. I was in the picture, and she actually took it."

Not every photographer found immediate acceptance at *Arizona Highways*, a fact that should encourage new talent struggling for recognition. In most cases, it was like the experience of Peterson, who recalls sending pictures to the magazine in the early 1950s. "They weren't very good."

The breakthrough for Peterson was a photo feature on beavers. Carlson pronounced the work "tremendous photography" but urged him to expand the brief article he had written. The first result was a cover story in 1953. The others were calls to Peterson for beaver stories from *National Geographic* and more than a half-dozen other magazines, suddenly hungry for nature pictures.

Wayne Davis, then a brash 19-year-old who had just exposed his first box of 10 sheets of the old 4 by 5 Kodachrome 25, remembers a sobering reception at the *Arizona Highways* office.

"Raymond (Carlson) placed my first offerings on a light table beside some super photographs by Esther Henderson in 5 by 7 size and some of Josef Muench's 4 by 5s. This was a most effective method of teaching a kid, still wet behind the ears, how very bad his work really was.

"I think he had those photographs there on purpose. I learned a lot just by looking at them. It was the lighting, mainly. They were both masters of using light to mold and bring out the image they wanted."

The visit, however, brought some encouragement and a request for some black-and-white photography of the Show Low area. That, in turn, was followed by a half-page color image of Monument Valley which was published in the magazine's

December 1948 issue and, says Davis, "I was on my way."

Jerry Jacka, too, recalls the cockiness of youth when he took his first 4 by 5 black-and-white prints to the magazine. Growing up on a ranch in the New River area, encouraged by a high school teacher who gave him use of a school camera and a key to the darkroom, Jacka had a single goal—to get one picture published in his favorite magazine.

"I just figured there was no way in the world that *Arizona Highways* could refuse this fantastic photography," he says. But there was, and it did. Not until he was in his mid-20s, working in forensic photography for the sheriff's office, did Jacka succeed in selling a landscape of the Painted Desert. His color portfolios and books, specializing in Indian art and artifacts, have made him one of today's most recognized *Arizona Highways* photographers.

A graphic designer who had learned and practiced a little photography at the old Thunderbird Field near Glendale during World War II, Bob Markow became interested in shooting horse shows and weekend rodeos. So it was a collection of his horse photos that first interested *Arizona Highways* after the war. Markow's wife made a story out of his notes on horse shows and they had a collaborative effort published in 1946. "She was quoted in several magazines as an expert, but actually she didn't know one end of a horse from the other."

But the photo feature led to other assignments for Markow, almost immediately plunging him into color photography. Shooting scenics, selling what he could, Markow built up a studio business in Phoenix, going on into commercial photography, laboratory work, and the photo supply business in a big way.

Almost naturally, son Paul Markow grew up to be an *Arizona Highways* contributor in his own right. From his earliest recollection, "sitting in the sink when I was four years old, rocking the tray to agitate the developer," to later chores such as painting floors and washing the cyclorama in his dad's studio, Paul says he was "brainwashed."

Reversing the direction of most photographers, he says, Paul started in commercial photography, then grew to love the fine art aspect more. Along the way he was represented in *Arizona Highways* with a half-dozen covers and such varied features as western fashions, Arizona jewelry, a San Juan River trip, and Arizona State University football training at Camp Tontozona.

A reminder that even the best can experience rejection comes from Carlos Elmer. After making his first magazine sales—two photographs in a 1939 *Desert* magazine contest, which earned him $5 apiece—Elmer took a box of prints on Havasupai Indians to

(ABOVE) One of the magazine's most noted scenic photographers believes that "The Brave Poppy" perhaps says more than any of her other published images (December 1949). ESTHER HENDERSON

(INSET) A champion Arabian stallion shows off for a feature on "Showing Horses" (November 1946). BOB MARKOW

(RIGHT) "Red Rocks, Oak Creek Canyon"
provided a view of the Doodlebug
Ranch in Sedona, now the site of the
Poco Diablo Resort (June 1945).
ESTHER HENDERSON

(ABOVE) Black-chinned hummingbird on a
hollyhock, probably on his last feeding for
the evening, was frozen in time for an
Arizona Highways front cover by a pair of
noted bird photographers (February 1952).
HARRY L. AND RUTH CROCKETT

Carlson. Coincidentally, there were plans for an Indian issue.

"I saw that gleam in an editor's eye," Elmer remembers. He shared that issue with photographers Barry Goldwater and Josef Muench.

But the gleam wasn't always there, and Elmer remembers images that didn't sell.

"The only time, though, that I felt glad about being rejected was when I heard Ansel Adams commenting on rejection of a Death Valley photo. I thought, 'My God, even Ansel gets rejected!'"

The association between Ansel Adams and *Arizona Highways* is a particularly interesting one.

Adams was officially introduced to the magazine's readers in its May 1946 issue, which had his dramatic Grand Canyon skyscape on the front cover, and a two-page spread of Lake Mead in a color portfolio inside, along with work of Josef Muench, Herb McLaughlin, and others. In fact, though, Adams' work had been in the magazine previously that year, including a Monument Valley scene in March and a view of Walpi village on the Hopi Indian Reservation in April.

Carlos Elmer, a trove of information about the development of *Arizona Highways* who is always ready with praise for other lens artists, makes a telling comment about Adams in connection with that Monument Valley image.

"One photographer told of shooting fifty 4 by 5s in a day at Monument Valley. Ansel Adams went to Monument Valley and was there a day and a half before he exposed his first sheet of film. His was a classic."

Adams and Raymond Carlson quickly established a rapport that was advantageous to both the photographer and the magazine.

In November 1951, Adams wrote to the *Arizona Highways* editor about plans to publish a series of regional books utilizing thousands of black-and-white negatives lying in his files, along with new images which he would photograph. Shunting aside any false modesty, Adams wrote: "I have a far-flung reputation now which I am anxious to cash in on in a thoroughly dignified and profitable manner."

His proposal, in brief, was that *Arizona Highways* put up some of the necessary travel and expense money, in return for pictures and articles to be developed along the way by Adams and his associate, Nancy Newhall, both a writer and a recognized authority on photography.

"As editor of the magazine, I have never been as proud as when I have had the opportunity, on rare occasions, to present your work," Carlson wrote back. He listed Arizona subjects in which he was especially interested, but left himself some obvious negotiating room on the terms of payment.

The terms apparently were ironed out to everyone's satisfaction, for by the following February Adams had sent Carlson portfolios on Canyon de Chelly and Sunset Crater, together with some suggested page layouts, technical notes which would be fascinating to serious photographers, and a sizable list of ideas for future photo stories.

(LEFT) "It's Playtime in Navajoland" captures a light moment at an encampment in Monument Valley (December 1956). JOSEF MUENCH (BELOW) "Reflections of Navajo Land and Life, Monument Valley" was a back cover image (January 1974). ALLEN C. REED

(FOLLOWING PANEL, PAGES 52 AND 53) "Navajo Weavers at Work"; mother and daughter work while a younger child waits quietly in a cradle board, photographed near Chinle (August 1957). GEORGE HIGHT (PAGES 54 AND 55) Earth and sky become one in this strangely somber, other-world view of Monument Valley (June 1979). ALLEN C. REED

Additional color photos and Newhall's texts were in the *Arizona Highways* office by May 1952, and in June (when Adams' Canyon de Chelly portfolio was published), Carlson was writing to Adams and Newhall confirming plans to publish a layout on Tumacacori, as well as other color material. This lengthy letter examines in detail more than a dozen comments, criticisms, and projects being discussed with Adams. A couple of anecdotes will suffice to show the relationship that had evolved.

First, Newhall had suggested a story on the mission at San Xavier del Bac for the *Arizona Highways* Christmas issue. Noting that, by the time he received her letter in late June, the Christmas issue was already virtually closed, Carlson wrote to her:

However, as I suggested over the telephone to Ansel, you two, if you have the material together, ... should submit this story, first, to Life *[magazine] for a Christmas story. Please understand that if any material that you have proposed to work up for us would have greater sales through some other magazine, we would not at all be offended. I realize that these other magazines pay much more than we do and we would be the first to cheer to know that other publications were presenting some of your things. As far as I am concerned, I am simply amazed that other editors have not seen the possibilities as* Arizona Highways *sees, in presenting the Adams-Newhall series.*

However, in talking to Ansel about this over the phone, he felt that his loyalty, of course, was to us and that we should have first crack at the San Xavier story. That is not, by any means, a proper attitude. We want you to make as much money as you can on this southwestern material and, by all means, if anything is salable by you two to another publication first, do not feel that we, in any way, will be offended.

The second story demonstrates Adams' scrupulous attention to detail and his deep concern for the integrity of his work. The letter from Adams that initiated Carlson's response is not available, but the editor responded with these words:

I have noted Ansel's minor criticisms on the two features that we have, so far, run. I agree with you, one photograph should not be inset in another as we did in the Canyon de Chelly story. Also, we will not jump pages on a story. We will keep the story intact. It just happened that because of space limitations, we were cramped with the Sunset Crater story. However, it will not happen again. Incidentally, all layouts will be submitted to Ansel before running, so if there is any criticism, that criticism should be voiced then and there and any [changes] made. In that way we will not have any minor criticism after the article has been published.

In the same letter, Carlson noted an Adams suggestion that *Arizona Highways* use a better grade of paper to achieve better reproduction, and expressed his hope that an experiment with a different kind of ink would enhance the printing process.

Arizona Highways obviously knew what a treasure it had in the work of Ansel Adams and was willing to do virtually anything necessary to protect its interest!

(LEFT) "Fiesta of San Xavier"; Tohono O'odham (Papago) Indian acolytes carry an image of St. Francis of Assisi, one of the photographic highlights of a landmark picture story on Mission San Xavier del Bac (April 1954).
ANSEL ADAMS

(ABOVE) "Ecce Homo — The Suffering Savior." Sunlight from star windows in the great dome of San Xavier's West Chapel illuminate the figure (April 1954). ANSEL ADAMS (FOLLOWING PANEL, PAGES 58 AND 59) With "Monument Valley," Adams joined other photographers in providing an eight-page color portfolio entitled "It's Spring Again" (March 1946). ANSEL ADAMS

In August of the same year (1952), Adams sent Carlson 228 black-and-white prints, with a promise of another batch "in a day or so." A subsequent letter promised that Adams would keep a basic collection of at least 150 prints in *Arizona Highways'* hands at all times, with "fresh things" to be sent as replacements for any that were published. More projects were listed for development by the eager Adams, who obviously was just as delighted as the magazine with their arrangement.

The Adams-Newhall feature on San Xavier del Bac finally materialized, although the team had to overcome considerable reluctance on the part of the Franciscans at the mission. One friar professed that he wouldn't give "even the Pope" the interview time that was requested. But the artistry of the published piece mollified the cleric, who described it as a "symphonic opus on Bac."

"What sheer delight for the eye, what melody for the ear—now soft and sweet with romance, now mighty and resounding with epic grandeur," he wrote, going on to give Adams and Newhall what undoubtedly was the most effulgent praise in his lexicon—"the most Franciscan people I have met outside the Order."

In the case of Adams, Newhall, and Mission San Xavier, *Arizona Highways* unquestionably reaped benefits from the diplomacy and the sheer brilliance of a pair of contributors to the magazine.

Many other photographers have noted a reverse phenomenon. The fame and reputation of *Arizona Highways* has come to guarantee an open door and a welcome to photographers at work. The fact is that it is known and welcomed virtually everywhere.

"Wherever I've gone in the world—and I've been all over the world," says Barry Goldwater, "all I've had to do is go to a newsstand, and there's *Arizona Highways.*"

Like all artists, *Arizona Highways* photographers have always been firm individualists. The uniqueness of each shows the most, as one might expect, in his preferred choice of subject matter.

Josef Muench, for example, has concentrated on scenics. Rarely do people intrude into his images—except for the Navajo Indians, for whom he has had a special affinity. Ray Manley, on the other hand, seems to enjoy involving people in his scenes, as long as they fit the theme. But both photographers, Manley says, are fairly "static" imagemakers, "seeing a scene as nature made it."

"Compose it the best, get the best possible light, but don't minimize the main subject," Manley says. Telephoto shots, he believes, tend to portray an untruth.

(ABOVE) "Walpi; Study of a Hopi Village" led into a chapter reprinted from Walter Collins O'Kane's newly-published book, "The Hopis: Portrait of a Desert People" (August 1953). ANSEL ADAMS

Navajos always played a major role in Goldwater's photography, particularly the black-and-white portraits which have commanded so much respect. Although he professes a certain disdain for color, one of Goldwater's outstanding images for *Arizona Highways* involved two little Navajo girls—and was in color.

On a mid-January day, Carlson called Goldwater to request a picture of two Indian girls tending sheep in the snow. The snow had gone by then, but a week later, Goldwater was at his Rainbow Lodge trading post and awoke to find a fresh fall on the ground. He walked about a mile down the road and encountered two Navajo girls with their sheep.

The photo was on the front cover of *Arizona Highways'* historic, 52-page 1946 Christmas issue, the first all-color issue of any nationally circulated consumer magazine in the United States.

Some of the most distinguished Indian portraits, both Navajo and Hopi, to appear in *Arizona Highways* were the work of Joseph H. McGibbeny. The tremendous respect which McGibbeny had for his Indian friends was returned. Among Navajos, he was known as Hosteen Kismus (Mr. Christmas), in appreciation for the relief he rounded up for reservation residents after a devastating drought in 1939.

McGibbeny's deep interest in Navajo and Hopi culture stemmed from 1921, when he attended University of Arizona summer classes in Flagstaff. Besides his color portraits, he contributed to the magazine rare photographs and first-hand accounts of ceremonials seldom witnessed by non-Indians. His "Hopi Butterfly Dance" was the front cover of the July 1953 issue, and his last appearance in *Arizona Highways* was in 1959, another account of a sacred ceremonial documented by his own photography.

"Among both professional and amateur workers, photography must be inspiring or degenerate into drudgery," McGibbeny wrote in one article. "Only by exposing each sheet of film with the feeling that perhaps the resulting picture will be your masterpiece can this inspiration be maintained. Only by choosing a subject that completely excites your interest can you hope to attain the feeling of something photographically worthwhile. For me, that subject is the Navajo."

A scenic photographer in Arizona without a copious and varied file of saguaro cactus images is like an egg without salt. One who confesses to favoring saguaros above all else is Dorothy McLaughlin, although she has enjoyed photographing Indians and her first *Arizona Highways* entry was a color back cover of a sailboat on Canyon Lake.

Dorothy is the wife and teammate of Herb McLaughlin, and they often shared photo credits in *Arizona Highways*. In 1971, an entire issue was devoted to the couple and their work.

Her often-published image of saguaros silhouetted against the sunset on a hundred-degree evening still lingers as a highlight of her career. The photograph preserves the memory of a thick stand of saguaros, north of Phoenix, that no longer exists.

Wayne Davis concentrated entirely on scenics, seldom straying from northeastern Arizona—east of the Grand Canyon and south

(FAR LEFT) "Cabin in the Snow," photographed on a January day in Oak Creek Canyon, illustrated the photographer's article about photographers, "You've Got to Go Back to Get the Good Ones" (September 1955). CHUCK ABBOTT (INSET) Looking specifically for Navajo children with their sheep in the snow, the photographer lucked into a late-season snowfall and a chance encounter on the Navajo reservation. "Blessed Are the Meek" was the front cover on the historic *Arizona Highways* first all-color issue (December 1946). BARRY GOLDWATER

to the Salt River Canyon. And he always came back to Canyon de Chelly, even traveling through the canyon by wagon with his children to shoot a 1959 *Arizona Highways* color portfolio.

"It is a great place—the canyon, the Indian people," he says. "It hasn't changed through the years; it's just like it was 40 years ago—isolated, no development."

Although Willis Peterson has published many beautiful scenic images in *Arizona Highways* and elsewhere, wildlife photography has pursued him relentlessly throughout his career—probably stemming from his Tom Sawyer boyhood on the mountain slopes near Colorado Springs.

Birds, beavers, alligators—all have been subjects for Peterson's loving approach to nature None provoked debate like Arizona's curious little kangaroo rat. Carlson had adamantly rejected Peterson's suggestion of a story on the subject.

"There will be no rats in my magazine!" the editor declared.

Peterson did what he refers to now as "the unthinkable"—calling on Carlson at home to pursue the subject. Reluctantly looking at the pictures Peterson brought with him, Carlson studied and studied them, as the photographer recalls it, finally saying: "I see what you mean."

Peterson's photo feature, "Speck–The Kangaroo Rat," appeared in the October 1960 issue of the magazine.

The contrast from the sweeping scenes of spectacular Arizona to the relatively miniature kangaroo rat sums up, in a way, the photographic span of *Arizona Highways*. The magazine has always portrayed not only the awesome majesty of the Grand Canyon, the wild beauty of Organ Pipe National Monument, and the lives of the creatures that roam forest and desert, but also the interplay among all the creations of nature, mankind included, that make up what we call Arizona.

In his fifth year as editor, Raymond Carlson described what he saw as the mission of the publication then entrusted to him.

This humble journal dedicates itself to the task of telling you something of one corner of America, this land of ours called Arizona. We will speak of roads and where they lead, and we will tell you something of the people who live along those roads. We will bring you tales of long ago, and we will have you meet some of our neighbors. We'll invite you to come in and "sit a spell." And most of all, these pages will reflect our pride in our land and our pride in America, of which we are all a part.

The mountains, the desert, the forests, the water, the people of Arizona . . . all have been portrayed in timeless images through the 65-year history of *Arizona Highways*, fashioned by photographers in whose creative minds and hands craft has become art.

In the words of one of them, "*Arizona Highways* is admired whether because of an interest in photography, or for the Arizona scenery itself. It is the envy of photographers everywhere."

It is the photographers whose timeless images have made it so.

(FAR LEFT) "Storm Light on Canyon Buttes," photographed at Mather Point on the South Rim of the Grand Canyon, captured a glimpse of dramatic sunlight near the close of a gray winter day. As an inside front cover, it helped introduce the photographer's roundup of four seasons in Arizona (October 1962).
DARWIN VAN CAMPEN
(LEFT) These images accompanied the photographer's article on a remarkable creature, the kangaroo rat (October 1960). WILLIS PETERSON

THE TRADITION
Grows

Massive natural forces at work, sometimes in violent collision with one another, sometimes in peaceful transition, have thrust, and carved, and shaped the land form that man has arbitrarily circumscribed and called Arizona.

Subterranean fury created the mountains and high plateaus. Canyons were carved by water and sculpted by the wind. Rocky debris was milled down to sand and soil; trees and plants sprang from seed and reproduced.

Man came; first the nomad hunters and basket makers, then the cliff dwellers, followed in turn by pastoral peoples and raiders who preyed on them. Conquistadores and priests were the vanguard of Europeans, leading the way for miners and cattlemen. Others came to exploit the resources, but in increasing numbers they succumbed to the beauty. Finally, they came simply to see the land, to marvel at it, to love it, and to live on it.

Shapes and colors awed viewers of the Colorado Plateau, etched and slashed by canyons. Occupying the northern third of Arizona, it encompasses the indescribable majesty of the Grand Canyon, the Painted Desert, Monument Valley, the Colorado River and its tributaries. The surface is barren in spots, bejeweled with waterfalls and turquoise pools in others. The San Francisco Peaks, reaching upward to 12,643 feet, seem to anchor it to the sky, and highland forests of ponderosa pine, spruce, and Douglas fir splash the mountainous terrain with multiple shades and hues of green.

In a band stretching across most of the state's width, defined approximately and in part by the Mogollon Rim, mountain evergreen forests interspersed with oak, juniper, aspen, and piñon provide living space for hundreds of varieties of living creatures. Man, often the enhancer rather than the aggressor, has dammed mountain streams and added lakes to forest glens.

Arizona's image to many outsiders, the desert country spanning much of its southern area, is punctuated by islands of semi-isolated mountain peaks and ranges. Nature's loving accommodation with aridity manifests itself in cactus and desert plants of myriad sizes and shapes, topped with colorful blossoms in the appropriate season. River bottoms, often dry, hoard their fertility only to lavish it generously when the inevitable runoff comes. And the wildlife — mammals, insects, reptiles, birds in

(ABOVE) A double exposure silhouettes cacti against Baboquivari Peak, (May 1980).
DAVID MUENCH
(FOLLOWING PANEL, PAGES 68 AND 69) View from South Rim of the Grand Canyon accompanied a special issue, "Welcome to Flagstaff Country" (June 1982). DAVID MUENCH
(PAGES 70 AND 71) Geological structures in the back country of Petrified Forest National Monument are seen from Kachina Point (February 1983).
DAVID MUENCH

dozens of varieties — thrives on the bounty of the land.

Portraying and preserving these vast and varied scenes of Arizona, along with remarking on the role of man in his chosen environment, has been and continues to be the special mission of *Arizona Highways* magazine.

Through photographic images, created by photographers with a particular affection for this land we call Arizona, *Arizona Highways* has, through 65 years of publication, amassed a treasury to lavish on those who share that affection.

The time when primal forces were shaping Arizona has a personal grip on some of the photographers who have shaped *Arizona Highways* through the years. One in particular is widely-acclaimed David Muench of Santa Barbara, California, who developed a love for the landscape while traveling with his parents, Josef and Joyce, as they photographed and wrote for *Arizona Highways*.

After studying at the University of California at Santa Barbara and the Art Center School in Los Angeles, and from a beginning in commercial photography in which he learned how to work with clients, Muench says, he has "moved toward portraying the landscape as it was before man came; the mystery of it.

"It's a personal way of finding myself and relating to the global orb we're on," he continues. "What draws me is the wild and mysterious in nature — plant and rock, the open spaces, fine detail in landscape, not too much animal life. I look for the shape and form of things. In some of the rugged country, it's like the planet is here with nobody else, and you just dropped in."

Arizona Highways, Muench believes, is uniquely able to portray the cultural diversity of the region. He sees its role as "addressing the strength and power and beauty of this land and the part we are of that land; it should be a spokesman for the land and the people living on the land."

Even occasional fatigue is forgotten in the "sense of discovery and awe" that returns to Muench when he is in the field. He admits to a feeling of dread when he was in the summer heat of southwestern Arizona, photographing for a new *Arizona Highways* book, *Eternal Desert*. Muench recalls that he "saw Cabeza Prieta and the Yuma area and I was just agog; I could have stayed there for a week, even with all the heat."

As with Muench, the work itself is motivation enough for many photographers of *Arizona Highways*. Some, closely tuned to nature, frankly hope their craft may have a beneficial effect in preserving the landscape against man's encroachment. One such is Jack Dykinga of Tucson, who turned his back on journalistic photography after winning a Pulitzer Prize with *The Chicago Sun-Times* and became a wilderness guide.

"I have a philosophical tie to the wilderness, in addition to the obvious vocational tie," says Dykinga, who used to "sort of salivate" while viewing the early landscapes of Josef Muench in *Arizona Highways*. "Environmental issues will be the issues of the '90s, and wilderness advocacy is the larger part of my interest and my market."

Dykinga still is likely to tell a story through a scenic image. An example is a Monument Valley photograph published in 1987 — a tiny bush which had been spun countless times by the wind, leaving a circular track in the sand. The viewer knows both the place and what has been occurring in that place before he arrived.

Wilderness preservation and resource management — what he calls the "land-use ethic" — also preoccupy Californian Jeff Gnass. Fascinated by the work of Ansel Adams, piqued by

(LEFT) Buffeted by changing winds, a tiny bush leaves its mark in the sand. In the background stand the line of "dancers" on Yei Bichei Mesa and the Totem Pole in Monument Valley (May 1987). JACK DYKINGA

photography during his participation in a Navy Antarctic expedition, Gnass is drawn particularly to the Sonoran Desert. The "grand landscape" is his favorite format, and people seldom intrude on the image.

"I look at my photography to express my feelings about these values," says Gnass. "If I'm successful, my photographs should expand people's understanding of a place, whether a mountain range or a canyon."

Jerry Sieve, who trained in photography at Glendale Community College under longtime *Arizona Highways* contributor Willis Peterson, explains his interest in preservation by saying: "Many of the images I have photographed cannot be duplicated, because the landscape has been destroyed."

From selling cameras in Cincinnati to using them in Arizona, Sieve was influenced by *Arizona Highways* and made his first real sale of professional work to the magazine. He likes to play with the slight distortion that exists around the edges of a wide-angle image, seeking drama rather than an absolutely faithful recording of nature.

"There is a certain power and feeling that you get in the Southwest," says Sieve, explaining his move westward. "The landscape is . . . surreal. People in other parts of the country don't believe the light . . . here; they say it doesn't exist, but they just don't understand it."

Land shapes and forms fascinate all scenic photographers, and Arizona's have particular interest for Peter Kresan. A geology teacher at the University of Arizona, Kresan brings from that scientific discipline a special way of looking at detail, patterns, textures. The result is reflected in images he has contributed to *Arizona Highways*.

"My background in natural history helps me tremendously," says Kresan, who became involved with photography only after moving from Connecticut for graduate work at the UofA. "I like to think I see things there that other people don't. I really can't separate photography from geology; I use a photographer's eye in geology and a geologist's eye in photography."

Not surprisingly, he believes the desert has produced his best camera work, although he has produced lovely images of fall colors in the White Mountains and the Chiricahuas.

Gary Ladd says he "went nuts" over cave exploration and photography at the same time while living in Missouri, and soon realized the dramatic images that he could produce while in total control of lighting, as in the depths of a cavern. Ladd now lives in Page so that he can be surrounded by the country he has come to love, particularly Glen Canyon and the Grand Canyon.

"The sandstone wilderness areas surrounding Lake Powell are extremely important to me," says Ladd. His wandering includes extended exploration of the Grand Canyon, where Ladd and his camera have covered up to 250 miles of off-trail hiking in a month's time.

Actually, Ladd's introduction to *Arizona Highways* was in a

(LEFT) Hauntingly beautiful Superstition Mountains, known as "Slanting Mountains" to the Pima Indians, are the state's most popular Forest Service Wilderness. This image illustrated a feature on hiking (June 1985). JERRY SIEVE

(ABOVE) Rolling grasslands below the Santa Rita Mountains were included in a special issue on the Tucson area (February 1986). WILLARD CLAY

(FOLLOWING PANEL, PAGES 76 AND 77) Lightning display during summer storm over Kitt Peak Observatory in 1972 became one of the magazine's most-requested prints for framing, and was reprinted in its 50th anniversary issue (November 1973, April 1975). GARY LADD

quite different area of Arizona — at Kitt Peak Observatory in southern Arizona. His spectacular, wide-angle image of a lightning display over the observatory occupied a two-page spread in 1975 and helped lead him into professional photography.

Another photographer who rarely uses people in his images — seldom even a man-made structure — is Tucson native Willard Clay. Marriage took Clay to Illinois, but he returns to Arizona for at least two photographic expeditions a year. Like David Muench and others, he strives to show pristine nature as it existed before the impact of man.

"This is becoming more and more difficult," says Clay. "It almost confines us to the national parks and monuments. Photographers are almost like the elk herds; we're getting pushed deeper and deeper into the wilderness."

Clay is a photographer who aims to capture what he calls the "decisive moment," perhaps the only instant when that particular image could be photographed. His scene of lush, waist-high grasslands below the Santa Rita Mountains, following a season of record-breaking rainfall, may never be duplicatable.

Being in the traditional "right place at the right time" was no accident. He keeps detailed notes on his shoots — the lens, filter, light conditions, time of day, etc. — and also on what he plans to shoot in the future when conditions are just right. Although Clay says Dykinga works in an opposite style — looking for what he can find rather than planning each step — the two often camp together and work together.

Tucson photographer Randy Prentice borrowed a quotation from another professional to express a philosophy similar to Clay's: "Photography is the art of being there."

A product of Pima College and the University of Arizona, Prentice knows pretty well what he will find in the Tucson area, and when to find it. Although he is a desert-dweller, he loves photographing "green-water areas." Away from his home base, he also stresses the value of scouting. In the Grand Canyon, for example, he might take a few "obligatory pictures" the first evening, while carefully watching the light to determine what he wants to photograph on ensuing nights.

Nevertheless, Prentice admits he will go into the field "without a picture in my head." One he didn't scout was an image of San Xavier del Bac, which succeeded in capturing architectural details of the mission through a series of its arches. Deceptively simple, it was shot with no complementary weather conditions — just the clear, blue sky as background.

To many readers and to many professionals, Ray Manley epitomizes *Arizona Highways* photography. He also is one of the most versatile of photographers. In his many images published in the magazine, viewers find vast scenic landscapes, Indians in their natural environment, cattle herds on the move, cowboys grouped around a campfire, magnificent sunsets. The common element for which he strives is truth. Readers will seldom, if ever, see a telephoto image with Ray Manley's credit; the scene doesn't actually exist that way.

"Anticipation" is a key word in Manley's approach to photography. Even in a fairly static landscape scene, he says, "you must consider what might happen if the sun should burst through five minutes before sunset — and be ready for it." The photographer, according to Manley, must continually analyze. There will be a sunset tonight; will it be just good or will it be spectacular? "Don't just photograph a bucking horse," he admonishes. "You must think: 'What if . . . ?'"

(LEFT) Ancient bristlecone pine was included in a 16-page excerpt from the photographer's museum exhibition, "The Glory of Nature's Form" (November 1976). WILLIS PETERSON

(FOLLOWING PANEL, PAGES 80 AND 81) Destination for hundreds of pilgrims each year, Mission San Xavier del Bac rests serenely in the desert southwest of Tucson. Two-page spread introduced feature, "Pilgrimage to San Xavier" (November 1986). RANDY PRENTICE

Manley, who has photographed sunsets all over the world, says southern Arizona is *the* place to capture sunsets on film. Moreover, he has analyzed the reason: Clouds build up over the Santa Catalinas and Baboquivari Peak; as the sun sinks and lights the clouds from beneath, the hot, dry desert expanse to the west prevents clouds from forming, so the sunlight is not blocked out. The result: colorful cloud patterns, lit from beneath.

Willis Peterson, professor and photographer, also stresses the importance of foresight. In wildlife photography, which has been an important part of Peterson's body of work, he has found it crucial to "educate yourself to all the possibilities. Anticipate the moment," he cautions. "It's there and then it's gone."

Anticipation can be a question of place just as much as one of time, according to Herb and Dorothy McLaughlin, Phoenix photographers who have chronicled scenes and events of Arizona as a team for many years.

"Where can you get a Phoenix skyline against a spectacular sunset?" Herb asks. The answer for them lay in continued scouting in an urban area with which they already were intimately familiar. The result was a prime location — the hilltop Wrigley Mansion, now called the Mansion Club, near the Arizona Biltmore. Armed guards escorted them to the top, where only one spot seemed to offer the perfect framing. After 36 exposures in only three minutes, the McLaughlins had two images that met their criteria. One of them turned out to be the wrap-around dust jacket photo on their book, *Phoenix, 1870-1970.*

Other *Arizona Highways* photographers also see and shoot in very personal ways. James Tallon, a former Grand Canyon tour guide, claims to be "like tuna — they roam around and take whatever they find; I just go out and shoot everything."

With a large stock file of scenics, Tallon now usually goes for wildlife. Campgrounds are a favorite site, as birds and squirrels come in to scavenge on food scraps. A 1985 *Arizona Highways* silhouette of a perching cactus wren was photographed from a Tallon-devised camera mount on a moving car as he cruised through Tucson Mountain Park.

Wildlife photography also is the primary emphasis of Robert Campbell, although he shoots landscapes and loves to film lightning. "I got tired of shooting animals; I decided I wanted to take pictures of them instead," the ex-hunter explains.

During a bad winter on his Texas ranch, about 1976, Campbell saw some rare whooping cranes fly in. Despite a 104-degree fever, he donned a snowmobile suit and went out with a Polaroid camera. The resulting film image: "Some little white dots." Determined to do whatever it took to produce good photographs, Campbell soon was winning awards. His experience as a rifle champion permits hand-held photography, even with a heavy 600-mm telephoto lens, on a self-designed camera stock.

His first published image in *Arizona Highways* in 1986 was of a butterfly. More reminiscent of his effort with the whooping cranes is a photograph of a coyote in a snowstorm. Campbell saw the

(LEFT) Coyote hunts during a winter storm near Tucson (February 1986). ROBERT CAMPBELL (ABOVE) A cactus wren in Tucson Mountain Park pauses just long enough to illustrate article, "Courage in a Cactus Patch" (October 1985). JAMES TALLON

storm moving in over Saguaro National Monument, grabbed a varmint caller and an old bedsheet for camouflage and went to work. The result was a full-page photo in *Arizona Highways*.

Ken Akers of Phoenix has a strong background in sports photography, and not surprisingly considers himself primarily a "people photographer." Rodeo and cowboys are growing as his main interest, one where the "anticipation" mentioned by other photographers is of great importance.

"What interested me is that moment when the cowboy is not really on the horse, but is not yet in control of the steer," says Akers of a 1989 rodeo action shot.

The image illustrates how Akers thinks of fast-moving events. "In rodeo, someone in the stands gets to watch the whole thing, but there are many small moments within that sequence. I like to isolate those special little moments so that people can see them and study them. I just get one crack at it."

The same attitude characterizes Akers' approach to landscapes. "I tend to see things in what I call 'widgets,'" he says. "Where Jerry Jacka might be shooting a very broad landscape, I would be photographing a very small part of that setting. I like breaking it into segments."

Los Angeles-based Kaz Hagiwara is another *Arizona Highways* contributor, like Peter Kresan, who began using his camera to record subjects on geology field trips and soon expanded into scenic landscapes. Land formations still attract Hagiwara to Arizona and neighboring states, his expeditions fitting into the schedule of his commercial photography business.

His 1980 sale of a Grand Canyon image to *Arizona Highways*, "a magazine I had always admired so much," convinced him that his future lay in professional photography.

Photographing the Grand Canyon is recognized as a serious challenge even by most newcomers, and it never loses its magnetism, even for such veterans as Carlos Elmer, a Kingman resident. He shuns artificial light to the point of claiming that "when the sun goes down, I'm out of business." Nevertheless he has a moonlit image from Mather Point on the South Rim that has helped his *Grand Canyon Country* book go into its 14th printing.

Elmer tells of seeing a tourist couple drive up to the one of the popular South Rim lookout points. The man jumped out of the car, sprayed the Canyon from left to right, top to bottom, with an 8-mm movie camera, then called to his wife, who was still in the car: "Myrtle, I've got the whole thing!"

"I don't think the Canyon gives up its secrets that easily," Elmer remarks. "It's a tough subject. I already have a trunkful of pictures, but I can't resist it. Often it's me versus the Canyon, and I lose!"

For Kathleen Norris Cook, a commercial artist who was "not even one of your serious amateurs" as a photographer when she moved to Phoenix in 1977, sale of an image of Toroweap in Grand Canyon helped launch a photography career. "I always find something new and wonderful to experience, especially in the inner gorge," Cook says. "That is one of the most spiritual experiences I've ever had."

The mystical lighting achieved by a Japanese photographer influenced Cook's work to the point that she waits for special, weather-induced lighting effects before exposing film. Trying to catch nature at its most unusual, she says, "I rarely pull out my camera on a clear day."

Another Canyon image by Cook, in the Nankoweap area, grew out of an assignment to shoot a series within the Canyon, all of the same scene, to indicate passage of time. The assignment was for a record album cover, but one exposure made on the same

(LEFT) View of the Inner Gorge of the Grand Canyon near Nankoweap Mesa (December 1985). KATHLEEN NORRIS COOK (FOLLOWING PANEL, PAGES 86 AND 87) A moment of action is captured during a University of Arizona rodeo at Old Tucson (February 1989). KEN AKERS

expedition added to Cook's own *Arizona Highways* album.

Wisconsin resident Tom Algire, inspired by the work of Ansel Adams, David Muench, and others, has always had a deep interest in Arizona.

Shooting "just a pretty picture" isn't enough. "I want to get the feeling that it is all balanced, that everything is in place." He may involve man-made features, such as barns or fences, but no people inhabit the scenic world of Tom Algire.

He recalls seeing a grove of aspen trees across a side canyon on the North Rim of the Grand Canyon, and thinking it just might be a possible shot. The uncertainty — not knowing whether he could bushwhack his way to the area, whether he could find a camera angle once he got there, or even if he could find a place to set up tripod and camera — illustrates what scenic photographers face in the field. Once he got there, "I had no more doubts; I had found it. I knew that nobody else had ever been in exactly that spot." The image appeared in a 1983 issue of *Arizona Highways*.

Like many imagemakers, veteran Phoenix photographer Dick Dietrich would choose the Grand Canyon and Monument Valley if he had to narrow down his favorite areas of Arizona. But a view of Grand Falls on the Little Colorado River is a special one among his many contributions to *Arizona Highways*.

"I was there in the late afternoon, waiting around to get that golden light on it just as the sun was setting," Dietrich recalls. "Then, with that warm light, the scene just kind of came alive."

Dietrich believes the scene "has to come together" to be successful. "Often it may look great to the eye, but it isn't going to photograph well. You may have to wait for a different time of day, or a different season, to put the elements together; or just the lighting can make a difference. I try to lay my mind open to what I find. A lot of times I go back to a place and ask myself, 'Can I take a different approach?' I look at it again.

"I've felt that I had a knack for recording nature, which seems to have proved fruitful for me. I like being out there, facing the challenge of coming up with a nice shot. Challenges: that's what life is all about, isn't it?"

Arizona's incredible light inspires all outdoor photographers. "That light is God's work," says the versatile Jerry Jacka, "not something some lab technician has conjured up."

Jacka, acclaimed for his Indian jewelry, pottery, and basket portfolios, but just as likely to turn up in the magazine with a grand scenic panoroma or a wildlife image, believes that too few people understand what he calls the "fine art-ism" of *Arizona Highways*.

"Photography has evolved in the magazine from documentary to a fine art," he says. "A painter can go to Sedona or Oak Creek and do a beautiful job; take out the power lines or change a roof. But a photographer has to have all the elements in place, plus a sensitivity to light and an imagination, and then has to capture it all with one snap of the shutter."

An avid trout fisherman, Larry Ulrich edged into photography seeking a means to finance his love of the outdoors. He has sold his own prints on the streets of San Francisco and Berkeley, published calendars with his own work and, with his wife, produced a coffee-table book, *Arizona's Magnificent Wilderness*, now nearing a sell-out of its third printing.

To Ulrich, a "landscape" could be an image in Downtown Los Angeles as well as Arivaipa Canyon, one of his favorite Arizona haunts. Seeking "very clear imagery," devoid of distractive elements, Ulrich analyzes a scene, picturing it mentally at a

(LEFT) Claret cup hedgehog cactus was among images in a Grand Canyon portfolio, "Temple of All Nature" (December 1986). TOM ALGIRE (FOLLOWING PANEL, PAGES 90 AND 91) Autumn afternoon scene from the same portfolio (December 1986). TOM ALGIRE (PAGES 92 AND 93) The Grand Falls of the Little Colorado River are equal in height to the more famous Niagara Falls (August 1977). DICK DIETRICH

different time of day, another season, a different light, using map and compass along with his camera, and doing a great deal of homework to minimize surprises in the field.

He also benefits from another pair of eyes, those of his wife Donna, who is with him in the field about 95 percent of the time. It was she who spotted the brilliant reds, oranges, and greens in an area along Oak Creek, about two miles above Sedona, which became "Streamside Garden," published in a 1984 issue of *Arizona Highways*, and in at least two books.

When in the Sedona area, Ulrich often spends time with another *Arizona Highways* photographic team, Bob and Suzanne Clemenz. Bob Clemenz, who found landscape photography a welcome relief from his darkroom-bound photomural business, saw Sedona for the first time in 1950, after a photo tour of Monument Valley and Grand Canyon.

"It took me a while to get back here to live," Clemenz says. But his first *Arizona Highways* sale, in 1964, was a double-page spread of Sedona from the Schnebly Hill Road.

The rear window of the Clemenz home has a beautiful view of one of the area's more striking landmarks, Cathedral Rock. Among scenic calendar publishers, Cathedral Rock usually sells even better than the Grand Canyon, Clemenz finds. A striking image of the formation, published in a 1981 issue of *Arizona Highways*, was taken by Clemenz on a cold November morning. With fall colors on the ground, and the sun rising behind the towering rock spire, there is a mist rising off Oak Creek that gives the image an ethereal, almost unworldly quality impossible to describe in words.

Probably nobody has done more than Sedona's Bob Bradshaw to capture on film the wonders of that photographer's paradise. From a free box camera he received on his 12th birthday, part of a 1930 promotion by Eastman Kodak, Bradshaw has progressed through one of the first 35-mm cameras on the market to large-format photography and back to 35-mm.

Working as a carpenter, Bradshaw literally saw the nation as a young man until he landed in Sedona, where he helped build the Sedona Lodge in 1946. That led to building sets for motion pictures being filmed in the area, and years of work as an extra and bit player, as well as a still photographer.

His first images in *Arizona Highways* added color to the 1950 Christmas issue — two Sedona-area scenes and a third photograph of a cowboy silhouetted against the setting sun. About the time those images were published, Bradshaw was initiating the picture postcard business which he still operates, featuring his own photography.

Typical of Bradshaw's artistry is a scene of Hartwell Canyon in which the sun hits the side of the mountain with such intensity that it almost appears to be on fire. It was shot from his ranch, with a 4 by 5 camera, and has been seen on postcards and on an *Arizona Highways* calendar, as well as in the magazine's issue of December 1966.

(LEFT) Bistort and snakeweed bloom in the highlands around Flagstaff (March 1982). JERRY JACKA

(ABOVE)The red rocks of Sedona wear winter white for a Christmas issue image (December 1982). BOB BRADSHAW (FOLLOWING PANEL, PAGES 96 AND 97) Colorful foliage decorates the floor of Oak Creek Canyon (December 1985). LARRY ULRICH (PAGES 98 AND 99) Soft morning mist hangs over Red Rock Crossing, on Oak Creek near Sedona (May 1981). BOB CLEMENZ

Tom Till is another photographer who learned about Arizona from the pages of *Arizona Highways*. In his case, it was while watching his mother, an Iowa schoolteacher, clip the magazine for classroom use.

A resident of Moab, Utah, Till spends much of his time on the road, photographing scenery everywhere from New Jersey to New Zealand. But northern Arizona continues to attract him, and he describes himself as "a Grand Canyon fanatic." Till is a professional river runner, among other things, and has photographed the Canyon many times from the special viewpoint known only to those with the white-water experience.

"I'm really attracted to weather," he says. "I'm excited by the dynamics of changing weather conditions — the rain, fog, clouds. Sunny days are great, but they can get a little boring."

One of his unusual views of the Grand Canyon, a scene of Cape Royal on the North Rim, resulted from what Till calls "the greatest assignment in the world." After spending about two years photographing the Arizona Strip, including a considerable amount of time along the North Rim, he had a major photo feature, including the Cape Royal image, published in *Arizona Highways* in September 1988.

Painter-writer-photographer Allen C. Reed, onetime Phoenix advertising executive now living in Page, describes his role as "primarily that of a communicator."

"I wouldn't draw anything that I could take a picture of; and if I can't get a picture that gets it across, then I paint it," Reed says. "My favorite type of feature has lots of pictures and captions, so you can see it and read it at the same time."

Notwithstanding that preference, Reed has had stunning single images in *Arizona Highways*, one of the most remarkable a solitary Navajo woman standing motionless beneath the arch of a spectacular rainbow, against a purplish-red sunrise. As often is the case, the image was partly a matter of chance. Reed had intended to pose the woman in front of the Totem Pole formation in Monument Valley. But a light mist was turning to rain, and he was becoming discouraged. Turning away from the scene, he saw the woman, patiently waiting for directions, with the rainbow curving above her. He grabbed camera and tripod, whirled around, set up quickly and snapped his picture — in the opposite direction from his carefully planned setup.

Reed's picture-stories and Dykinga's journalism background have company in the roster of the magazine's contributing photographers, among them Jeff Kida and Fred Griffin.

Griffin, who fantasized in elementary school about being a *National Geographic* photographer, and who remembers having *Arizona Highways* around his family's Texas home while he was growing up, considers himself an "editorial-style" photographer. Environment is his main interest, but he has shot fashion, skydiving, off-road motoring, and country fiddlers. Skilled at reading a topographical map and "a hard-core backpacker," Griffin will hike (or ski) nearly anywhere to fulfill an assignment.

It is his environmental interest that came to the fore in a major *Arizona Highways* spread on Topock Gorge. For that photo series, Griffin spent nine days in a canoe, along with two camera bodies, six lenses, and a tripod. His greatest worry: being swamped by passing motorboats.

Kida, whose photography interest was whetted by a teacher in Bolivia, where his father was stationed in the U.S. Foreign Service, studied photography at Arizona State University. Awarded an internship at *Arizona Highways* on the basis of a color portfolio he submitted, Kida says he "probably hung around

(LEFT) Sunrise at Cape Royal, on the North Rim of the Grand Canyon, was a front-cover image (September 1988). TOM TILL (FOLLOWING PANEL, PAGES 102 AND 103) Cowboys in bunkhouse at Spider Web, one of the CO Bar ranches, appeared in a special issue, "The Working Cowboy" (June 1981). JEFF KIDA

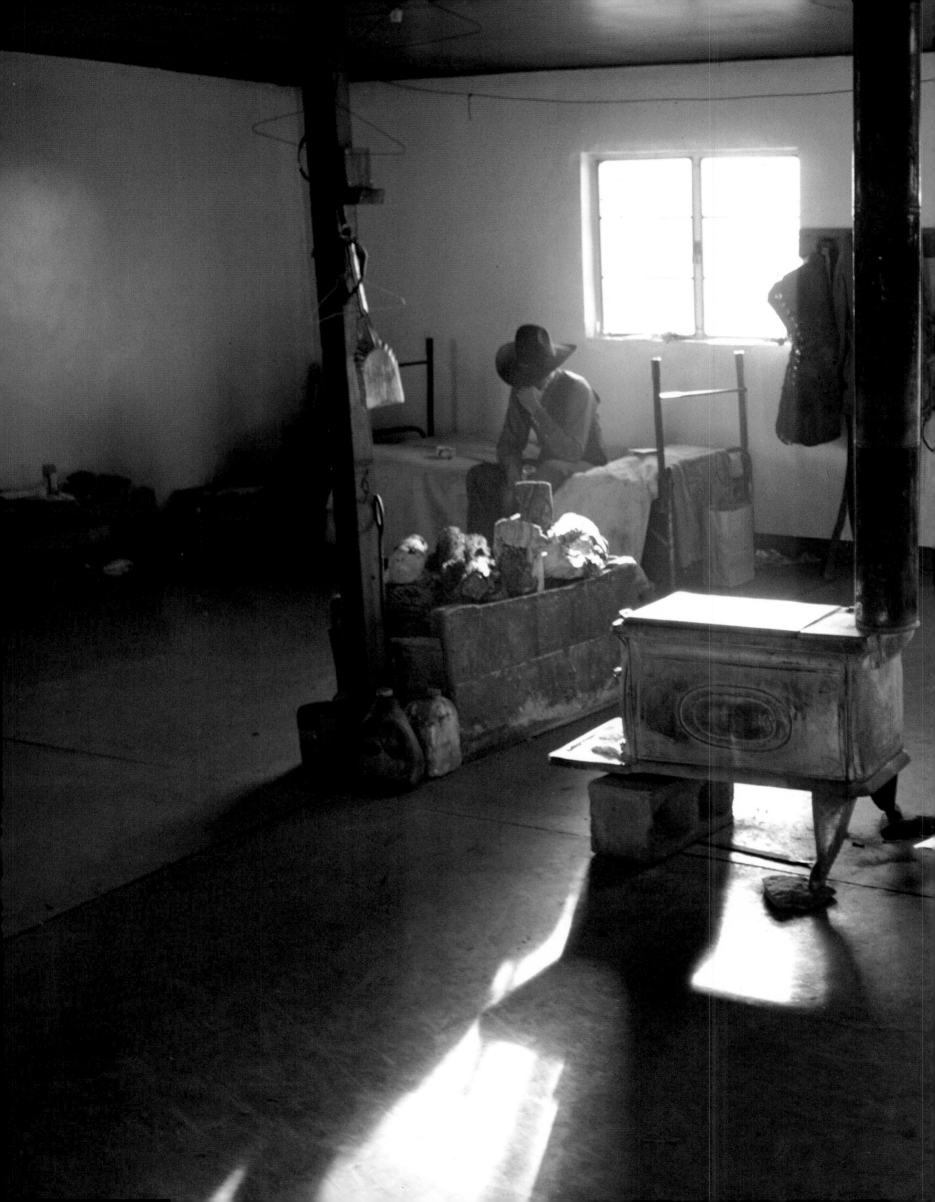

longer than they had intended."

Learning from magazine staff members and studying the work of Josef Muench, Jerry Jacka, and others, Kida developed his skills. "I'm not in the scenic league with them," he says. "I lean more toward people stories, like the one on working cowboys."

Despite that preference, one of his more memorable *Arizona Highways* images was his "University of the Future," an exterior of the new Arizona State University West, a multiple exposure with the building, the moon, and aircraft landing lights swooping through the frame.

"The images themselves are reminders of enjoyable times working on stories," says Kida. "*Arizona Highways* evokes a good feeling with people. It opens doors.

"I like to make nice images, and to try each time to make it better. It's being competitive with yourself. You do it for the readers, but you aspire to a level you haven't attained before."

Christine Keith, one of the magazine's newer regular contributors, was lured into color from classic black-and-white photography in the fine art tradition, and from 35-mm to large-format photography by the opportunity to work for *Arizona Highways*.

After studying with Jay Dusard at Prescott College, and shooting documentaries in Mexico and Thailand, Keith had an image of Zoroaster Temple in the Grand Canyon published with a 1978 article in *Arizona Highways*. When she learned the magazine had dispatched two "real" photographers to complete the job, she said to herself: "I could have done that."

Publication of her image of the desert near Pinnacle Peak in spring bloom in 1983 led her to decide that, "Maybe I can do this." In 1985, she photographed most of a special *Arizona Highways* on Prescott — "a wonderful opportunity." After two years off for professional study, leading to a national Leica award, and a stint in newspaper photography, Keith is in the early stages of a promising career.

Herb McReynolds is a rarity: a person who combines two very different vocations and who probably will keep it that way. As Dr. McReynolds, he specializes in emergency medicine in Tucson; as Herb McReynolds, he hikes with backpack and camera through the mountains and canyons of Arizona and Alaska.

As a youngster in Virginia, McReynolds learned about photography and Arizona from his grandfather, a darkroom amateur and a Federal Reserve Bank president who brought copies of *Arizona Highways* back from western business trips. When the opportunity came, McReynolds left his medical practice in the east and came to Arizona's White Mountains, living in Pinetop and practicing on the Apache Reservation.

Reversing the role of the broad landscape photographer, he assembled a portfolio of macro lens imagery that was published by *Arizona Highways* in October 1988, under the title "Nature Through a Close Focus Lens." McReynolds says the images gave

(LEFT) Don Arnulfo Pinuelas, still drawing full pay as a cowboy at 100, was featured in an issue on Nogales (February 1981).
J. PETER MORTIMER

(ABOVE) "Welcome to Prescott Country" included this scene on Prescott's famed Whiskey Row (April 1980).
J. PETER MORTIMER

him an opportunity to "isolate the smaller essences of each scene—to get the feel of the small scene."

The images by Frank Zullo seen by *Arizona Highways* readers could not be further removed from those ultra closeups. A former motion picture and television documentary photographer, Zullo worked his way back into still camera work by putting together professional slide shows. He free-lances in all areas of photography, and has gravitated toward nature and outdoor subjects. But a special affinity for night sky photography has brought his work into public focus.

The magazine's 1985 Christmas issue carried its first two Zullo images — hawks soaring against a large moon, and a view of cactus silhouetted against the Milky Way.

The technical problems in such photography are formidable and, not surprisingly, many of the images are composites. "People have a tendency to say, 'Oh, yeah, it's trick photography,'" Zullo says. "But I try to make it look as natural as possible."

A love for astronomy dating from his childhood, infinite patience, and a willingness to experiment are key ingredients in what some viewers refer to as Zullo's "nightscapes." Beyond that, he seeks images with "a spiritual outlook; photographs that make you feel like something else is there, just beyond what we actually see in life. I hope to capture some of the magic in nature."

Perhaps without intending to, Jeff Kida struck on a key factor in the emergence of *Arizona Highways* as a unique artistic element in the world of magazine publishing, when he spoke of "being competitive with yourself." Editors and contributing photographers, through 65 years of *Arizona Highways*, have followed a credo that has become a legacy: "Aspire to a level you haven't attained before."

Nature provided the visual magnificence of Arizona. Man has changed some of it, but much remains inviolate, majestic, shaped into timeless beauty. For those who have seen and want to remember; for those who have been unable to see for themselves; for those who treasure a moment in time captured forever, the magazine and its architects have aspired to do more and do it better with each succeeding issue.

Some of those early black-and-white images seem raw and unsophisticated today. But they were breathtaking artistic successes at the time. The genius of the imagemakers still shines through. Lenses, shutters, and other camera equipment have undergone great technical advances. There have been strides in reproduction techniques—color separations, presses, paper, inks. Today's full-color, laser-scanned images, reproduced by high-tech equipment on paper stock not dreamed of 65 years ago, are possible only because of the determination of those photographic artists to reach new levels of timeless images.

(LEFT) Ponderosa pines are dwarfed by canyon walls in the West Fork of Oak Creek Canyon (March 1987).
CHRISTINE KEITH

(ABOVE) A mosaic of ivy leaves with one displaced red leaf was found for macro-lens feature, "Nature Through a Close-Focus Lens" (October 1988).
HERB McREYNOLDS
(FOLLOWING PANEL, PAGES 108 AND 109)
Halley's Comet is viewed from the Superstition Wilderness shortly before dawn (February 1988). FRANK ZULLO

IMAGES TO MATCH

A TIMELESS LAND

(ABOVE) Sunlit cliffs are mirrored in
calm waters of the Colorado River
(December 1986).
LARRY ULRICH

PRECEDING PANELS:
(PAGES 112 AND 113) A storm at sunset
in northeastern Arizona was part of
a special issue, "In Coronado's
Footsteps," tracing the explorer's path
(April 1984).
JERRY JACKA
(PAGES 114 AND 115) Morning dew
sparkles over thousands of spider webs
in a White Mountains meadow
(December 1987).
BOB CLEMENZ
(PAGES 116 AND 117) Autumn colors
abound against the tapestried cliffs of
Canyon de Chelly (December 1983).
DICK DIETRICH
(PAGES 118 AND 119) "Visions of
Eternity"; view of Four Peaks was
included in a holiday portfolio,
"America's Premier
Greeting Card" (December 1983).
JERRY SIEVE

(FOLLOWING PANEL, PAGES 122 AND 123) Horses are unloaded for spring roundup on the Babbitt Ranch, introductory image in a special issue, "The Working Cowboy" (June 1981).
JEFF KIDA

(ABOVE) "Sedona by Stormlight" was a key visual element in a color portfolio, "Colors — The Music of the Eyes" (August 1980).
DICK CANBY

(ABOVE) The article, an unabashed
play on words, "In Rodeo, Cowboys
Get All the Breaks" provided a behind
the chutes look at the life of the rodeo
cowboy. (August 1984).

KEN AKERS

(FOLLOWING PANEL, PAGES 126
AND 127) A saddle bronc rider bursts
out of the chute during action in
Scottsdale's Parada del Sol Rodeo.
"The Rodeo Cowboy" feature was
included in a special issue, "The
Working Cowboy" (June 1981).
JEFF KIDA

(ABOVE) Adrenaline and determination
show in the face of this cowboy as he
prepares to explode out of the chute
(August 1984).
KEN AKERS

(RIGHT) Autumn paints the Chiricahua Mountains in southeastern Arizona (October 1983).
DAVID MUENCH

(FOLLOWING PANEL, PAGES 130 AND 131) The San Francisco Peaks, Arizona's highest mountains, are a dramatic backdrop from "The Season of the Photographer" (October 1986).
LES MANEVITZ

(PAGES 132 AND 133) Winter morning mists rise from Padre Bay on Lake Powell (December 1987).
GARY LADD

(ABOVE) The Miller Peak Wilderness in southern Arizona was portrayed in an issue largely devoted to wilderness lands in the state (March 1986).
JERRY SIEVE

(ABOVE) Pat Goodnight, eagle dancer

from Taos Pueblo, performs at

O'odham Tash celebration

(February 1987).

JACK DYKINGA

(FOLLOWING PANEL, PAGES 136 AND 137) "Sudden Storm in Navajoland" was included in 18-page color portfolio, "This Scenic Land" (January 1979).
DICK DIETRICH

(ABOVE) Dennis Alley Jr., all-state basketball player and a professional Indian dancer since he was 3, is a member of the Wisdom Dancers, a family group (May 1989).
FRED GRIFFIN

(RIGHT) Snowstorm engulfing the Santa Catalina Mountains near Tucson made a striking back cover image (January 1987).
JACK DYKINGA

(ABOVE) Saguaros and rainbow came together on a hillside near Tucson (December 1985).
ALAN MANLEY

(RIGHT) Ruins of the Mission San Jose de Tumacacori are now part of Tumacacori National Monument (September 1987).
JACK DYKINGA
(FOLLOWING PANEL, PAGES 142 AND 143) Wild horses roam the Cerbat Mountains near Kingman. Many of them are descended from 150 head purchased in 1870 by Hualapai Indians with money earned scouting for the Army (February 1988).
PETER ENSENBERGER

(ABOVE) Master weaver Gusta Thompson displays her highly prized coiled basketry (July 1977).
JERRY JACKA

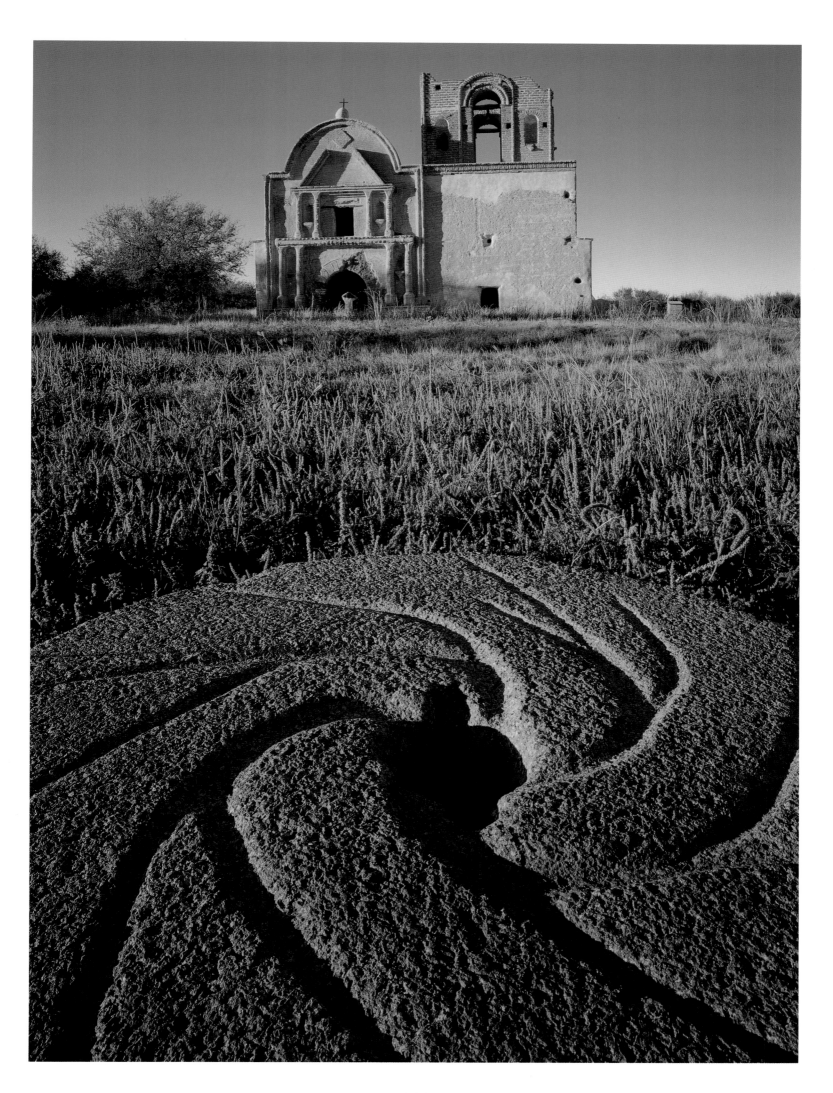

(LEFT) "Hopiland" was part of a special issue, "The Hopi Tricentennial," marking 300 years since the normally peaceful Hopi Indians threw off Spanish domination (September 1980).
JERRY JACKA

(FOLLOWING PANEL, PAGES 146 AND 147) "Walpi at Sunset" shows the ancient Hopi Indian village on the southern tip of First Mesa, with the San Francisco Peaks on the horizon and, at far right, Sacred Corn Rock on the slope of Second Mesa (September 1980).
JERRY JACKA

(ABOVE) Hopi girl's hair is being styled by her aunt in the butterfly, or maiden's whorl, once worn by all eligible unmarried Hopi maidens but now a purely ceremonial adornment (September 1980). JERRY JACKA

(LEFT) A spectacular view of Havasu
Falls, on the Havasupai Indian
Reservation, shows its turquoise pools
of travertine (September 1984).
CARLOS ELMER
(FOLLOWING PANEL, PAGES 150
AND 151) Blue Mesa in the Petrified
Forest illustrated an article on
"Arizona's Other National Park"
(February 1983). DAVID MUENCH

(ABOVE) An editor's note in the 50th
anniversary issue of *Arizona Highways*
described this view of Havasu Falls as
"a favorite of art directors"
(April 1975).
WAYNE DAVIS

(ABOVE) "Buckwheat and Cinders"
helped tell the story of Arizona's
remarkable and varied land formations
(December 1981).
DAVID MUENCH

(ABOVE) "Delicate Flowers and Spring
Cactus" were photographed on Ajo
Mountain Drive (November 1979).
WILLARD CLAY

(ABOVE) Desert creatures leave their
trail in "Nature is the Artist"
(December 1971).
WILLIS PETERSON

(FOLLOWING PANEL, PAGES 158
AND 159) Beavertail cactus in bloom
were a highlight of "Gifts of the
Desert" feature (December 1987).
KAZ HAGIWARA

(ABOVE) The photographer spotted
"God's Dog: The Coyote" for his
feature, "Stalking Wildlife with
Binocular and Camera" (June 1985).
JAMES TALLON

(LEFT) "Spring Comes to the Forest
Floor" records changing seasons in the
high country (April 1986).
DAVID MUENCH
(FOLLOWING PANEL, PAGES 162
AND 163) Black volcanic rocks washed
down from lava flows are scattered
over sandstone near Sedona
(June 1986).
GILL KENNY

(ABOVE) Raptor captured on film in the
North Kaibab Forest for feature,
"Stalking Wildlife with Binocular and
Camera," has been variously identified
as a hawk of one species
or another (June 1985). JAMES TALLON

(ABOVE) A mud-crack mosaic pattern
forms in the dry bed of the Santa Cruz
River South of Tucson (April 1988).
RANDY PRENTICE

(RIGHT) The fantasy world of a slot
canyon near the Arizona-Utah border
has a supernatural aura
(December 1989).
MICHAEL FATALI
(FOLLOWING PANEL, PAGES 166
AND 167) A field in Apache-Sitgreaves
National Forest, near Springerville, is
ablaze with goldweed, locoweed, and
Indian paintbrush (December 1988).
WILLARD CLAY
(PAGES 168 AND 169) One of nature's
wonders, Rainbow Bridge, is
approached from a narrow inlet of
Lake Powell (December 1982).
ED COOPER

(ABOVE) Oblivious to traffic, Navajo
horses amble across the highway near
Bitter Springs, in a feature titled "U.S.
89 — The Ramblin' Road"
(April 1987).
JAMES TALLON

(FOLLOWING PANEL, PAGES 172
AND 173) An Avra Valley sunset made
a spectacular lead-in for a feature on
the "Tucson corridor," titled "Arizona
South" (January 1980).
PETER KRESAN

(ABOVE) In a daring maneuver
captured on film for a front-cover
image, two members of the Quadrille
de Mujeres precision drill team charge
toward each other at a full gallop, then
pull up with split-second timing
(February 1989). KEN AKERS

CONTRIBUTORS TO TIMELESS IMAGES
Date in italic is the year when contributor's first photograph appeared in Arizona Highways.

Abbott, Chuck
(deceased)
First contribution: 1947

Adams, Ansel
(deceased)
First contribution: 1946

Akers, Ken
Phoenix, AZ
First contribution: 1978

Algire, Tom
Merrill, WI
First contribution: 1984

Bradshaw, Bob
Sedona, AZ
First contribution: 1950

Campbell, Robert
Tucson, AZ
First contribution: 1982

Canby, Dick
West Sedona, AZ
First contribution: 1973

Clay, Willard
Ottawa, IL
First contribution: 1979

Clemenz, Bob
Sedona, AZ
First contribution: 1964

Cook, Kathleen Norris
Laguna Hills, CA
First contribution: 1977

Cooper, Ed
El Verano, CA
First contribution: 1968

Crockett, Harry L. & Ruth
Phoenix, AZ
First contribution: 1939

Davis, Wayne
St. Johns, AZ
First contribution: 1948

Dietrich, Dick
Phoenix, AZ
First contribution: 1961

Dykinga, Jack
Tucson, AZ
First contribution: 1982

Elmer, Carlos
Kingman, AZ
First contribution: 1940

Ensenberger, Peter
Tempe, AZ
First contribution: 1984

Fatali, Michael
Phoenix, AZ
First contribution: 1987

Goldwater, Barry
Paradise Valley, AZ
First contribution: 1939

Griffin, Fred C.
Seal Beach, CA
First contribution: 1985

Hagiwara, Kaz
Los Angeles, CA
First contribution: 1980

Henderson, Esther
Santa Cruz, CA
First contribution: 1938

Hight, George
Gallup, NM
First contribution: 1957

Jacka, Jerry
Phoenix, AZ
First contribution: 1958

Kegley, Max
(deceased)
First contribution: 1939

Keith, Christine
Phoenix, AZ
First contribution: 1978

Kenny, Gill
Tucson, AZ
First contribution: 1975

Kida, Jeff
Chandler, AZ
First contribution: 1978

Kresan, Peter
Tucson, AZ
First contribution: 1978

Ladd, Gary
Page, AZ
First contribution: 1972

Lowman, Hubert A.
Arroyo Grande, CA
First contribution: 1942

Manevitz, Les
Phoenix, AZ
First contribution: 1981

Manley, Alan
Tucson, AZ
First contribution: 1968

Manley, Ray
Tucson, AZ
First contribution: 1943

Bob Markow
Phoenix, AZ
First contribution: 1946

McGibbeny, J. H.
(deceased)
First contribution: 1946

McLaughlin, Dorothy
Phoenix, AZ
First contribution: 1962

McLaughlin, Herb
Phoenix, AZ
First contribution: 1946

McReynolds, Herb
Tucson, AZ
First contribution: 1982

Mortimer, J. Peter
Phoenix, AZ
First contribution: 1976

Muench, David
Santa Barbara, CA
First contribution: 1952

Muench, Josef
Santa Barbara, CA
First contribution: 1939

Peterson, Willis
Sedona, AZ
First contribution: 1953

Prentice, Randy
Tucson, AZ
First contribution: 1986

Reed, Allen C.
Page, AZ
First contribution: 1949

Sieve, Jerry
Cave Creek, AZ
First contribution: 1977

Tallon, James
Phoenix, AZ
First contribution: 1964

Till, Tom
Moab, UT
First contribution: 1981

Ulrich, Larry
Trinidad, CA
First contribution: 1984

Van Campen, Darwin
(deceased)
First contribution: 1966

Wallace, Norman G.
(deceased)
First contribution: 1933

Weber, Roger
Show Low, AZ
First contribution: 1988

Zullo, Frank
Mesa, AZ
First contribution: 1985

A southwestern bald eagle returning to its aerie above the Salt River was a front cover image introducing a series of rare and exciting photographs documenting the mating-parenting cycle of our national symbol (May 1988).

ROGER WEBER

ARIZONA

GOOD ROADS ASSOCIATION ILLUSTRATED ROAD MAPS AND TOUR BOOK

THE GRAND CANYON

CONTAINING PHOTOS OF ROADS, LANDMARKS, RESORTS, TOWNS, POINTS OF INTEREST AND DETAILED INFORMATION ON EVERY PART OF

THE WONDERLAND

ACCOMMODATIONS, SERVICE, SCENIC ATTRACTIONS AND RESOURCES

EXPOSED

Studio Photography by Ernst H. Weegan
Special Graphics Production by Ann Hermanson
Production Assistance DeLora Dellinger